READ ALL ABOUT IT!

DRUGS

EMMA HAUGHTON & JON REES

W

FRANKLIN WATTS

LONDON•SYDNEY

First published in 2000 by Franklin Watts
96 Leonard Street, LONDON EC2A 4XD

Franklin Watts Australia
14 Mars Road, Lane Cove
NSW 2066

Copyright © Franklin Watts 2000

Series editor: Rachel Cooke
Designer: John Christopher, White Design
Picture research: Sue Mennell

A CIP catalogue record for this book is available from the British Library.

ISBN 0 7496 3753 6

Dewey Classification 362. 29

Printed in Malaysia

Acknowledgements:
Cartoons: Andy Hammond pp. 14, 25; Sholto Walker pp. 16/17.
Photographs: Front cover: Format: main picture (Karen Robinson); Impact Photos: tr (Toby Key); Popperfoto: cra (Reuter/Pascal Rossignol), br (Dave Joiner); Rex Features: crb; Back cover: Format (Karen Robinson);
Insides: Format pp. 6 t (Karen Robinson), 9 b (Joanne O'Brien), 23 (Gillian Allard), 25 (Lisa Woollett);
Illustrated London News Picture Library p. 13;
Impact Photos pp. 3 tl (J. Hitchings), 3 b (Andy Johnstone), 6 b (Toby Key), 7 (Homer Sykes), 8 t (Piers Cavendish), 10 t (Vera Lentz); Penguin Children's Books pp. 3 tc, 22 t & b;
Photofusion pp. 4 (Stuart Saunders), 15 (Alex McCarren), 16 b (Chris Killick), 27 (John Southworth);
Popperfoto pp. 3 tr (Sportsphoto/Michael Mayhew), 5 (Reuters/Ian Waldie), 9 t (Reuters/Ian Waldie), 11 b (Reuters/El Norte de Monterrey), 12 t (Reuters/Arthur Tsang), 12 b (Reuters/Jerry Lampen), 20 l (Reuters), 20 r, 26 t, 28, 29 l (Sportsphoto/Michael Mayhew);
Redferns p. 8 b (Michel Linssen);
Rex Features pp. 11 t (C. Brown), 14 t, 18, 19, 21 t, 23, 26 b;
Ronald Grant Archive p. 21 b.

EDITOR'S NOTE

Read All About It: Drugs takes the form of a newspaper called *The Drugs News*. In it you can find a lot of articles about a lot of different subjects and many facts. It also includes opinions about these facts, sometimes obviously as in the editorial pages, but sometimes more subtly in a news article: for example in the article concerning the drugs in clubs (page 6). Like any newspaper, you must ask yourself when you read the book 'What does the writer think?' and 'What does the writer want me to think?', as well as 'What do I think?'.

However, there are several ways in which *The Drugs News* is not and cannot be a newspaper. It deals with one issue rather than many and it has not been published on a particular day at a particular moment in history, with another version to be published tomorrow. While *The Drugs News* aims to look at the major issues concerning illegal drugs and their abuse today, the events reported have not necessarily taken place in the past few days but rather over the past few years. They have been included because they raise questions that are relevant to the issue today and that will continue to be so in the future.

Another important difference is that *The Drugs News* has been written by two people, not many, in collaboration with an editor. They have used different 'voices' and, in some instances, such as the letters and the agony column, pseudonyms. However, the people and events reported and commented on are real.

There are plenty of other things in *The Drugs News* that are different from a true newspaper. Perhaps a useful exercise would be to look at the book alongside a real newspaper and think about, not only where we have got the approach right, but where we have got it wrong! Finally, we would like to thank Edward Ellison for permission to use his opinion piece on page 17 and Melvin Burgess for agreeing to be interviewed. Enjoy reading *The Drugs News*.

THE DRUGS NEWS

Foreign News   **10**

International drug trade worth billions

Profile   **22**

Melvin Burgess, author of *Junk*

Sport   **29**

Linford falls foul of drugs ban

WE STILL JUST SAY NO

Government refuses to change drug laws despite new report

The News Editor

The government has quashed police plans to make Britain's drug laws more liberal, which would have lifted the threat of imprisonment for the 70,000 people a year arrested for possessing cannabis, ecstasy and LSD.

A report from the Police Foundation said that penalties for cannabis do more damage than the drug itself. It called for cannabis to become a class C drug, removing the threat of imprisonment for possession. It also wanted ecstasy and LSD to become class B drugs, with no imprisonment and a maximum £1,000 fine for possession.

The government rejected the proposals to reclassify cannabis, ecstasy and LSD, saying it had 'a clear and consistent view about the damage which drugs can cause to individuals and their families ... the link between drugs and crime – and the corresponding need to maintain firm controls.'

FIRM CONTROLS

But Lady Runciman, who chaired the enquiry, said Britain's drug laws should reflect how much harm they actually do. 'When young people know that the advice they are given is either exaggerated or untrue in relation to less harmful drugs, there is a real risk they will discount everything else they are told about the most hazardous drugs, including heroin and cocaine.' ■

Drugs for sale on a counter in an Amsterdam 'café'.

POLICE TAKE CHILDREN TO DRUG DEN

Parents and teachers are up in arms about police plans to take 60 schoolchildren to cannabis cafés in Amsterdam's red light district as part of a new drugs education initiative. They are concerned that this will encourage the children to experiment with drugs rather than educate them about their dangers, as the police claim. ■

DRUGS: GOING DUTCH? READ MORE ON PAGE 14

A NATION OF JUNKIES

Home Affairs Editor

More than half the British population has experimented with illegal drugs at least once, according to astonishing statistics from the 1999 British Crime Survey.

The survey, based on 10,000 people, shows that drug use is steadily increasing. Cocaine, which is highly addictive, is now Britain's fastest growing recreational drug among 20-year-olds. Its popularity has spread since street prices halved and it became seen as the glamorous drug of choice for the rich and famous.

HEROIN CHEAP

Heroin, even more addictive and potentially deadly, is also spreading since prices have fallen. Another government study shows that in one area, two per cent of 13-14-year-olds have taken the drug.

But cannabis is still the most widely used illegal drug in Britain. Up to two million adults smoke it regularly, but it is also popular with the young – a third of 15-year-olds have tried it.

However, some drugs are becoming less popular. Use of ecstasy, associated with the dance and clubbing culture, appears to be falling. Deaths through solvent abuse are levelling off, due to the increased availability of other drugs and campaigns warning of the dangers of solvents. Also it seems fears of a US-style crack epidemic have not materialised.

The survey found that people are coming into contact with drugs and experimenting with them at a younger age than ever before. However, the heaviest users tend to be older, including the very rich, the very poor, and single professionals living in inner cities. ■

With cocaine popularity on the up, bank notes aren't just used to buy the white powder!

The Most Reverend Richard Holloway has radical views on cannabis use.

ADDICTION ON THE INCREASE

There were only 33 registered addicts in Britain in 1958; today there are more than 25,000. Whereas drugs used to be seen as an inner city problem, a 1998 police report detailed an 'epidemic' of heroin in small towns and the shire counties. Depressingly, inspite of three decades of harsh legislation banning the use and sale of heroin, you can now get it anywhere in the country. ■

PULPIT PUSHERS!

Church leaders say 'Smoke Dope!'

Several Scottish clergymen have provoked outrage by suggesting young people should be taught how to use cannabis.

The Most Reverend Richard Holloway, head of the Scottish Episcopal Church, believes young people should be taught how to use recreational drugs responsibly and moderately. Banning cannabis is akin to banning cream sherry, he says.

CREAM SHERRY?

'Something that people want to do in enough numbers and which does not harm others is not a crime. Some people for some reason like to drink cream sherry. We may not like it but we should not forbid it.'

His radical views are supported by Donald Macleod, of the Free Church of Scotland: 'I do think it is quite illogical and hypocritical to be trying to criminalise cannabis and at the same time to be advertising and packaging alcohol... Cannabis is no more destructive than alcohol.'

Not surprisingly, many are highly critical of their views. 'Cannabis is the first step down the rocky road to disaster,' insists John Orr, chief constable of Strathclyde, where over 100 people died from drugs in 1999. 'There is clear evidence that some of these people started on cannabis. They find that they just don't get the buzz out of it and move on to harder drugs.' ■

The drugs we are taking

These are the drugs most commonly used today, their usual form and how they can be taken. Most are illegal, but some can by prescribed by doctors, and solvents purchased. Magic mushrooms can be picked in the wild, but it is illegal to dry, sell or purchase them. ■

Drug	Usual form	How taken
Amphetamine/speed	powder or tablets	swallowed, sniffed, injected
Amyl nitrate	liquid	sniffed
Cannabis	brown/black resin or grass	smoked or eaten
Cocaine	white powder	sniffed
Crack	crystals	smoked
Ecstasy	pills	swallowed
Heroin	brown or white powder	injected, sniffed or swallowed
LSD/acid	tablets, impregnated paper	swallowed
Magic mushrooms	dried/fresh mushrooms	eaten
Sedatives/barbiturates	tablets	swallowed
Solvents	glue, lighter fuel, aerosols	inhaled

DRUGS IN CLUBS

Everyone wants to enjoy themselves on Saturday night, but just how safe is it to use drugs to have a good time? Research shows that ninety-seven per cent of London clubbers have taken drugs. Indeed, ecstasy, one of clubland's most popular drugs and used by 500,000 Britons every week, is now a £1 billion a year industry – more than the UK spends on tea and coffee. Other popular club drugs include amyl nitrate, cannabis, cocaine and LSD. Some clubbers even use prescription drugs, such as tranquillisers and Viagra, the drug used to treat impotence,

on the dance floor.

But there is increasing evidence that long-term use of ecstasy can cause brain damage which can lead to serious depression as users get older. Another study has found that the drug can trigger 'midweek blues' a few days after the weekend.

Researchers are also worried about people combining Viagra with other drugs like amyl nitrate, which together can dilate blood vessels and cause a dangerous drop in blood pressure, potentially causing a heart attack or stroke.

However, most clubgoers are unconcerned. 'You're

No worries! A young woman enjoys a good night out.

UNCONCERNED

always reading about this sort of stuff in the papers,' says Phil, 21, 'but it's one thing one week and another the next. I've never had any problems, and nor have my friends.'

Alina, 27, however, admits that she's had to drop out of

the club scene because of bad reactions to drugs. 'You can take ecstasy for months, years even, and it's great at first. But gradually you realise you just can't get your life together, and that even when you're taking the stuff you're not having such a good time any more. When I got like that I knew I just had to stop.' ■

Trade Valued

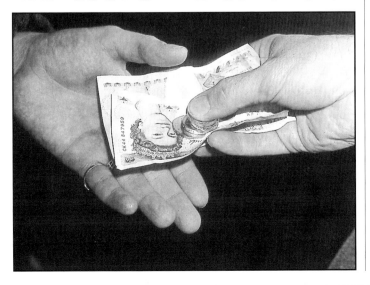

Shocking new government statistics show that Britain's drugs trade could be worth up to £8.5 billion – more than the country spends on fighting crime, and as much as a small country's total wealth.

The figures from the Office of National Statistics are the first official attempt to estimate the value of the drugs trade to the UK economy, and show the difficulty of trying to curb an

£8.5 billion changes hands for drugs – cash only, please!

underworld industry driven by huge profits. Although the authorities have seized more drugs in recent years, they stop only a small proportion of the drugs entering the country.

GLOBAL TRADE

Worldwide, drugs are worth around 8 per cent of legal trade, putting them in the same league as the textile, oil, gas and tourist industries. Only around 10-15 per cent of heroin and 30 per cent of cocaine is ever intercepted by police or customs. ■

Out of control

A new report raises worrying concerns about the policing of drug trafficking in Europe with relaxed border controls

Cannabis blocks confiscated by UK customs are burnt.

The abolition of internal border controls between countries in the European Union has opened the way for drug trafficking on a huge scale, and opened up European politics to corruption, says the Geopolitical Observatory for Drugs, based in Paris.

The Observatory's 1999 report also said that drug gangs have gained a foothold in political parties, police forces and courts in several EU countries, and said the EU's anti-drug policies were 'wishful thinking'.

The report described Spain, in particular, as an aircraft carrier for drugs, serving as the EU's main entry point for narcotics from all over the world, as well as the main centre for money laundering by the Colombian cocaine cartels.

The report has been greeted with dismay by European governments.

TOUGH PENALTIES

Such is the concern about drug crime in Europe that Prime Minister Tony Blair has call for tough minimum penalties imposed on all EU members for trafficking in hard drugs – dealers and smugglers currently face sentences ranging from one to 20 years in different European countries.

Blair wants to persuade countries currently applying to join the EU – Poland, the Czech Republic, Hungary, Slovenia, Cyprus and Estonia – to agree to cooperate with moves to curb drug trafficking and to adopt an agreed minimum sentence policy. ■

Cannabis cover-up

The controversy surrounding attitudes to soft drugs was highlighted when United Nations health chiefs suppressed a finding that cannabis is safer than alcohol or cigarettes. A World Health Organisation report published in December 1997 was to have concluded that even if cannabis was consumed on the same scale as the 'socially acceptable' cigarettes and whisky, it would probably cause fewer health problems, but the passage was scrapped at the last moment. ■

On top of the world

The drug most widely abused is cannabis, used by 2.5% of the global population. This equals about 140 million people worldwide. ■

Flying doctors

The British Medical Association estimates that 13,000 of its doctors have a drug problem. The statistics have raised concern about the easy access to drugs that doctors have as a result of their profession. ■

Could a cure for drug addiction soon simply mean a trip to the chemist?

Popping Pills for Addicts?

KICKING THE HABIT

Here are some more traditional methods of curing addiction. Could they become a thing of the past?

Cold turkey: Giving up heroin or cocaine suddenly and without support. It can bring on painful and distressing withdrawal symptoms, but some people do manage.

Rehabilitation: Clinics prevent addicts getting hold of their drug, while helping them through withdrawal.

Methadone: A legal heroin substitute, available on prescription. The dosage is gradually lowered until the user no longer needs it.

Talking cures: Counselling and therapy which helps addicts understand how their behaviour led them to drug abuse and find ways of controlling their habit. ■

Future generations who want to get over addiction to illegal drugs like heroin and cocaine may simply have to swallow a pill.

Scientists around the world are working on various legal drugs that may help combat addiction. Happy Mondays' star Shaun Ryder claimed that a new drug called naltrexone helped him overcome his 15-year heroin addiction. Naltrexone, used as a

Shaun Ryder

stomach implant, blocks the effects of opiates like heroin and reduces cravings for the drug. It also prevents addicts from getting high if they do take heroin again.

Another new drug, known only as BP 897, could help treat a wide range of addictions, including alcohol and nicotine. Experts believe it works by dampening the effect of signals that addicts associate with their habit and which can trigger further cravings,

such as the sight of a syringe.

In the US, trials have begun on ibogaine, a mind-altering drug refined from an African shrub, which brings on a hallucinatory trance. This seems to give people an extraordinary insight into their behaviour. After a 36-hour session with ibogaine, many addicts say their desire for heroin vanishes without withdrawal symptoms. Some experts believe it could also cure cocaine and alcohol addiction. ■

KEITH HELLAWELL

How does the government's drug tsar aim to tackle drug abuse?

Keith Hellawell talks to schoolchildren to find out their views on drugs.

Youngsters need honesty about the risks and pleasures of drugs, believes Britain's first drugs tsar Keith Hellawell – or rather the UK Drugs Co-ordinator and Special Adviser to the Prime Minister.

In his late fifties, this Yorkshireman's first contact with drugs was as a young policeman in Huddersfield, when he dealt with two local doctors who had died from a heroin overdose. At first Hellawell thought the police could combat drugs by prosecuting as many people as possible. But he gradually realised the hard-line approach was failing when local drug-taking reached epidemic proportions in the 1980s, with ordinary working people regularly taking crack, heroin and other substances.

Now Hellawell does not believe catching and imprisoning more users is the answer. Instead police should put more effort into education and prevention, he says, liaising with schools, prisons and social services.

Although Hellawell has been criticised for suggesting that children as young as four should be taught about the pleasures and dangers of drugs, he still believes young people need a clear message not to get involved. Parents and teachers should try to learn and understand more about drugs so they are confident in talking about them, he says, and they should not be too judgemental. 'One of the reasons people take them is for the buzz, but there's also curiosity, coercion, weakness and need. Society has to be more sophisticated about the message we give to young people.'

He also wants to set up US-style drugs courts which can send addicts for treatment. If they fail to keep up with the treatment and go back to drugs, they will then return to court for sentencing for their offence.

Hellawell has strongly supported the government's stand against changing the legal status of some drugs (see the headline article, page 3). He feels that to soften the law would make abuse even harder to control, not less so. Yet with increasing public pressure for reform, it may be that the drug tsar will have to think again. ■

A class of 6-year-olds in London are shown syringes and warned of their dangers.

A worker in Peru lays out coco leaves to dry, part of the process of making cocaine.

Billion Dollar Trade

Foreign Affairs Editor

Illegal drugs are now big business, making more money than some of the world's largest traditional industries, says a United Nations report.

The annual turnover of illegal drugs is now at least $400 billion – about 8 per cent of total international trade, and more than either the steel or car industries.

Despite police and customs' efforts, global production of drugs is escalating fast. The amount of opium grown for heroin has more than tripled since 1985 – most is produced in Afghanistan, Iran and Pakistan. Opium production in Afghanistan alone has soared from 400 tonnes in 1980 to 2,800 tonnes in 1996.

Cocaine production has more than doubled in the past ten years, the bulk coming from Colombia, Peru and Bolivia. In Colombia the amount of land under cultivation to cocaine has risen from 12,000 hectares in the early 1990s to 45,000 hectares in 1995.

ESSENTIAL INCOME

For many countries drugs are essential to the economy and provide work for many. In Mexico, the narcotics business is worth up to $32 billion a year, while in Pakistan illicit drug export revenues are estimated at $1.5 billion. ■

American High

Americans spend around $70 billion a year on drugs, including $38 billion on cocaine, $10 billion on heroin, and $7 billion on marijuana. Some 85 million people in the USA have tried an illegal drug.

In the light of these statistics, the US government is fighting back, spending $17 billion of public money on the anti-drugs war. This compares with Britain's mere £500 million, although the US problem is arguably larger.

Stopping the drugs entering the States is one of the major problems facing America's campaign, particularly when corruption is rife amongst their own customs officials. It is said drug barons will pay US customs officers $50,000 in cash for each truck they wave through – just a small slice of the $7 billion budget drug producers have for bribing officials. ■

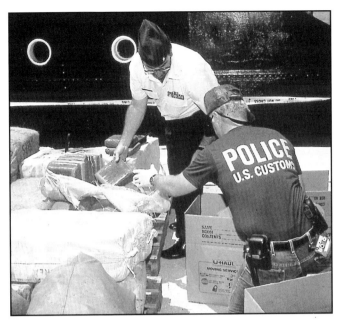

US customs officers check packing boxes for drugs.

HAWAIIAN HABILITAT

Hawaii seems an unlikely place for the toughest drug rehab centre in the world, but on the island of Oahu, Habilitat has offered a home and treatment programme for addicts for the last 30 years. Habilitat is a last chance for around 120 addicts. But whereas other treatment centres generally just involve a month's stay to help them get the drugs out of their system, Habilitat takes anything from two to six-plus years – as long as is needed for them to kick their habit once and for all.

Some of the inhabitants are here by court order in place of a prison sentence, but many are being sponsored by their families, to the tune of some £50,000 for two years. But it is worth it; Habilitat has a success rate three times higher than the national average for residential programmes.

Run by Vinny Marino, an ex-junkie from New York, Habilitat uses a combination of discipline and group therapy called The Games. These offer a safe environment where the addicts, known as The Family, can air their problems and the causes of their addiction.

But the centre is no cosy alternative to a prison sentence. The rules are tough and those who break them undergo punishments like having their head shaved. But there is nothing physical to keep people there; anyone is free to leave at any time. However, those that want to return have to literally beg to be taken back. ■

DEATH IN MEXICO

Three members of a Guadalajara drug cartel were shot dead on the street. Guadalajara is Mexico's second city and police suspect the deaths are part of a struggle between rival cartels for control of its drug trade. The two leaders of the Guadalajara cartel, Pedro and Oscar Luperico, are currently serving 13-year prison sentences, leaving a power vacuum that rival gangs are fighting to fill. ■

Holidays from Hell

Travellers must take care to make sure their exotic break doesn't last a lot longer than they expected, warns the Home Office.

In many popular holiday destinations, the penalties for being caught with illegal drugs are severe, including life imprisonment and even death. Countries which can impose the death penalty for drugs offences include Egypt, India, Malaysia, Singapore, UAE and Thailand.

BRIBES DEMANDED

Traffickers can plant drugs on tourists to get them across international borders. But travellers should also be wary of corrupt officials. One British couple who went to Goa, in India, had drugs planted in their rooms by police; when they refused to pay a £2,000 bribe they were given a 10-year jail sentence.

Even travellers who take drugs before they go abroad risk arrest – two Singapore residents were jailed for a year after traces of cannabis they had smoked three weeks earlier in Australia were discovered in a urine test.

Despite all the warnings some travellers do take the risk of drug smuggling. In 1993 Briton Sandra Gregory,

who had fallen ill while travelling in Thailand, met Robert Lock, who offered to pay her fare home if she would carry some heroin for him. Desperate she agreed, but the pair were arrested at Bangkok airport. They spent 3 years awaiting trial in a Bangkok jail. Lock was then acquitted, but Gregory was given a 25-year sentence.

After a pardon from the king of Thailand, Gregory served only 7 1/2 years of her sentence. On her release her advice concerning drugs (smuggling or taking) was simple: 'Just don't have anything to do with them'. ■

HOME OFFICE TRAVEL ADVICE

● Don't carry anything through customs for someone unless you know what it contains.

● Pack your own luggage and keep it with you at all times.

● If you use prescribed drugs, make sure you carry a prescription or a note from your doctor or hospital.

● Never purchase or take any drugs with you abroad, even if they are just for personal use.

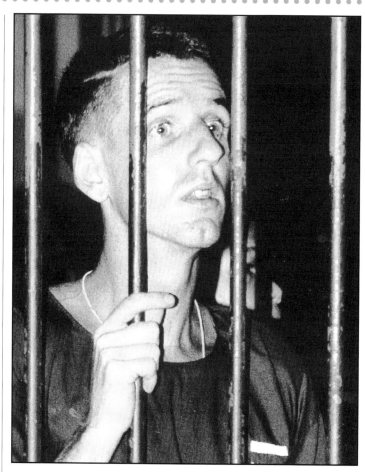

Robert Lock behind bars in Bangkok, Thailand.

RIGHTS FOR ADDICTS

The Netherlands' reputation for a liberal attitude towards drugs was shown once again at a demonstration in Rotterdam. Police helped this female drug addict to join the protest, which was mounted by addicts hooked on hard drugs. Their demands included more compassion for drug users and the right to work. ■

'Come along madam, the protest is this way...!'

A brief history of opium

We tend to think of drug abuse as a modern problem, but people have been experimenting with mind-altering substances for thousands of years. One of the most popular was opium, a drug derived from the same poppies as heroin.

As long ago as 4,000 BC, the Sumerians used opium for calming and pain relief, referring to it as Hul Gil, the Joy Plant. The Assyrians picked up the use of opium from the Sumerians, and in turn passed on the art of poppy cultivation to the Babylonians. From Babylon, it then made its way into Egyptian culture.

Opium gradually spread to Greece, Persia, India, Portugal and the rest of Europe. It was used by Europeans as a painkiller in pill form as early as 1527, and in 1606, ships chartered by Elizabeth I were instructed to purchase the finest Indian opium for transport back to England.

OPIUM WARS

By 1767, the British East India Company's import of opium to China reached a staggering 2,000 chests a year, effectively giving it a monopoly on the opium trade. In 1830, the British were getting through 22,000 pounds of opium, imported from Turkey and India, for medicinal and recreational use. Indeed it was considered so important that nine years later Britain declared war on China for the control of opium, resulting in the British take-over of Hong Kong.

Up until the late 19th century opium was sold as freely as alcohol today. In 1915, in the USA, there were over 150,000 opium addicts in New York alone. However, since 1878, when Britain passed the first Opium Act to try and reduce opium consumption, laws around the world have gradually tightened against opiate use. In most countries it is now illegal, except in medicine for pain relief, where its use is carefully policed. ■

In the 19th century, opium dens like this one flourished in London's East End.

GOING DUTCH

Story continued from page 3

The Education Editor

The issue of how drugs education should be delivered to children has been brought into focus once again by Thames Valley Police's new drugs education initiative. This includes taking 60 schoolchildren to Amsterdam drug cafés, where drugs such as cannabis are taken freely.

Bob Haynes, schools liaison officer for Thames Valley Police, believes that the expedition will give the teenagers a more rounded picture of drug use. Children learn best from their peers, he argues, and need good information to pass on to friends.

But many parents and teachers disagree. They believe the new approach is 'irresponsible' and will encourage children to experiment with drugs. 'Youngsters don't need to know all the effects a drug has on the body,' said one spokesperson for parents, 'They just need to be taught they are dangerous and how to say no.'

Bob Haynes says in response to the criticism: 'The more people know about drugs, the more they will understand they are not the answer to their problems. It also gives the children the chance to look at drugs from a different approach. It is up to them to make their own judgements about whether drugs should be legalised or not.'

The trip will follow a residential weekend and evening sessions giving information about drugs.

It is interesting to note that, despite their more relaxed drug laws, Dutch 15-year-olds are less likely to use cannabis than those in Britain. In addition, solvent abuse and glue sniffing is almost unknown in the Netherlands, and few young people there move on from soft drugs to harder ones. ■

A window for an Amsterdam café displays its wares.

What do you think?

We visited several Bristol secondary schools to ask young people what they think about the drugs education they receive.

Amy, 14

'Last year our PSE teacher invited a drug addict in to talk to us about what it was like being addicted to heroin. I was a bit nervous at first but he was really nice. It really made me think. I mean, he looked terrible and he said he had to spend over £200 a week to get enough to stop him feeling really ill. He really wanted to stop but he said it was so difficult.'

Jonas, 16

'We've learned about different drugs from books, you know, what things do to you and what the dangers are. It's a bit of a giggle, really, 'cos it's not like it's exactly news, is it? You're sitting there and wondering what the teacher really knows about drugs. I can't really see the point of banging on about it so much.'

Naseem, 12

'We had a policewoman came into the school once and she told us all about the law and drugs, and how you can get prosecuted, and how that could stop you getting a decent job in the future. I think that worried me more than all that stuff about how dangerous it is.' ■

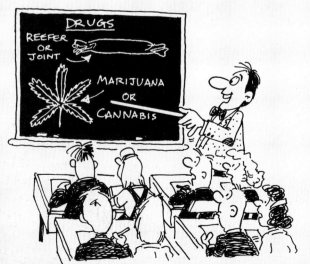

SNIFFER DOGS IN SCHOOL

Two boys sniffing solvents – they are among one in five British teenagers!

Bramhall High School in Stockport, Manchester, has at least one claim to fame – it is the first school in Britain to bring in sniffer dogs to search for drugs.

PRIVATE SECURITY

The searches, carried out by a private security firm, were authorised by headmaster John Peckham after talking to parents and staff. 'It is a statistical fact that between 10 and 15 per cent of all children have experimented with illegal drugs by the time they are 16, so the more we can do to tackle the issue, the better,' he says.

'Kids do things that are foolish and we feel that by having these searches we are providing another weapon in the armouries of those who want to say "No" to drugs. If they are offered drugs, this is another reason they can give for turning them down.'

During one search a 15-year-old boy was found to have a small quantity of cannabis, while another had traces of the drug in a cigarette packet. Both were suspended.

PARENT SUPPORT

The school also holds drugs education classes for pupils and awareness sessions for their parents.

One parent explained why she supported the school's policy: 'If it's a choice between having my child's rights infringed by a dog sniffing her bag or having some idiot trying to sell her drugs in the playground, I know which I will go for.' ■

Survey results

One in four 13-year-olds has taken an illegal substance, a government-backed drugs survey found recently. By the age of 15, more than half have tried at least one drug, usually cannabis. By their twenties, a quarter of young people will have tried cannabis.

The substance abused most after cannabis is solvents – it's estimated that one in five teenagers in Britain has sniffed solvents. ■

Editorial

FIGHTING A LOSING BATTLE

Few can doubt that the drugs war has been lost. The 23,000 prosecutions for trafficking in 1997 represent a small fraction of the drugs coming into the country. Jailing drug offenders evidently does not act as a deterrent; even those countries which impose a death sentence for drugs offences still have problems with abuse.

We all pay for this defeat. Heroin addicts typically spend around £10,000 a year on drugs, while crack users spend £20,000. Much of it comes from crime, which costs around £3-4 billion a year; drug offenders commit one in three burglaries and street robberies.

Despite this, the government spent two-thirds of its drugs budget in 1997-8 on enforcing the law, leaving just a third for drug treatment, prevention and education. Wouldn't taxpayers' money be better spent on attempting to get to the root of the drugs problem? Putting users in prison does not get them off drugs, but drug treatment programmes do. Studies show that for every £1 spent on drug treatment, more than £3 is saved in reduced crime.

BACK TO BASICS

But even treating addiction is not enough. We need to get back to basics. Education in schools has been proven successful in keeping kids off drugs but it is still an area of debate as to what form the education should take. Some people still seem determined to that the best way to educate people about drugs is simply to demonise and terrify.

However, it is worth remembering that one of the largest groups of drug users is the very poor. If we really want to win the drugs war, we need to tackle poverty and unemployment, not just punish people who use these substances to escape it. ■

Letters

Not criminals!

In reference to John Biggott's article last week on 'depraved and degenerate druggies', I would just like to point out that people do not take drugs because they have a 'criminal' mentality.

As a youth worker I find that people experiment with drugs for many reasons – curiosity, pressure from friends, unhappiness, boredom or simply to have fun. Prosecuting everyone who breaks the law is not the answer; accepting that drugs are now a common part of life and helping people deal with them sensibly is. Mr Biggott's attitude is as destructive as the drug-taking he criticises.

Yours, Alan Sound

What's your poison? Alcohol, cigarettes or illegal drugs?

Bitter experience

Many people will disagree with John Biggott's assertion that 'the road to hell is paved with cannabis', but I should know. I started on cannabis at 15, but soon found I was trying other drugs like speed, LSD and heroin. I've been a junkie for 13 years and just can't stop. If the penalties for drug-taking had been harsher, I might never have found myself in this position.

Yours, Ivan Abbitt

Legal drugs

Biggott by name, bigot by nature, it seems, since your columnist admits he enjoys smoking and drinking. What does he think nicotine and alcohol are? They are drugs, just like the 'evil' cannabis, cocaine and heroin he rants about – the only difference is that his preferred substances happen to be legal.

Yours, Jane Fury

IN MY OPINION

Edward Ellison, former Head of Scotland Yard's Anti-Drugs Squad

"Drugs should be legalised to protect our children"

As a former drugs squad chief I've seen too many youngsters die. I'm determined my children don't get hooked – which is why I want all drugs legalised.

In the seven years I spent at Scotland Yard's Anti-Drugs Squad, I saw first-hand the misery that drug abuse causes – the squalor, the wrecked lives, the deaths. I saw, and arrested when I could, the people who do so well out of drugs – the dealers, importers, and organisers. I saw the immense profits they make out of human misery. They run a hugely profitable business where the mark-ups are immense. They have a captive audience, and pay no taxes on their profits.

DRUGS-RELATED KILLINGS

Later, in the murder squad, I saw the drugs-related killings. I've also seen the knock-on crime – the muggings, break-ins and burglaries to which addicts resort to pay for their drugs. We have attempted prohibition. All that happened was the courts were clogged with cases of small, individual users, and a generation of young people came to think of the police as their enemies. There were no resources left to fight other crime. We then concentrated on the supply chain – the pushers – and let off end-users with a caution, but ended up with a high crime rate and huge profits for criminals.

DRUG USE IS GROWING

Prohibition has failed. Drug use is now part of the social life of around half our children. From cannabis to registered heroin addiction, drug use is growing. Each large police seizure merely drives up the price on the street, guaranteeing higher profits for the criminals.

Now I have two children at a vulnerable age and will do anything to keep them from the clutches of the drugs barons. I abhor drug abuse and criminal activity, I condemn a policy that profits criminals, and I am angered by the drug crimes that affect us all.

USE MARKET FORCES

So I say legalise drugs because I want to see less drug abuse not more, and I want to see the criminals put out of business. Let us use market forces to drive these criminals out of business. We can reduce demand by education. We cannot do it by policing. Lord knows we have been trying long enough.

Drugs that cost £1,000 on the street could be produced for just £1. That is £999 which would not be stolen from you, and go straight into the pockets of crime syndicates. Users getting their drugs from a legal source could access counselling, support and therapy – all the things they need to break dependency.

HIT WHERE IT HURTS

Legalising cannabis does not mean encouraging it, but the reverse. It means that parents and teachers can discuss it with young people openly. They will get education, not propaganda, and will be less likely to take it as a gesture of adolescent rebellion. The same applies to harder drugs.

If reputable companies like ICI could make and sell drugs there would be education, quality control and the price would plummet. The criminals would be hit where it hurts them most – in their pocket. They would have no more clients. We would truly drive them out of business. ■

OFFICE ADDICTS

The Business Editor

Forget the image of drug users as unemployed and unemployable – most people who use drugs are professional and skilled workers, says a new report from the Office of National Statistics.

Drug abuse costs British industry over £800 million a year, and can lead to poor judgement, lack of concentration, more days off work, more accidents and lower productivity.

Employers are gradually waking up to these facts, and how much it is costing them.

According to another government agency, the Forensic Science Service, one million UK employees face testing for illegal drug use. One in ten employees tests positive for illegal drugs, the FSS found, and this figure held true as much for the boardroom as the shop floor.

TESTING COSTS

Drugs testing is currently more common in certain industries, like transport, medicine, banking, heavy industry, the armed forces, or other professions where it is important for people to be clear-headed and healthy. Unfortunately, testing for drugs is expensive. Whereas an alcohol breathalyser test costs £10, drug samples have to be sent to laboratories and repeated if positive, and can cost as much as £100. London Transport alone spends a six-figure sum on drugs testing each year.

But the consequences for testing positive are varied, ranging from dismissal to just a note in a personnel file. While 90 per cent of companies have a smoking policy and 63 per cent an alcohol policy, few have one for drugs. ■

DRUGS IN THE BLOOD

Ecstasy and amphetamines will be out of the bloodstream within 48 hours, cocaine and opiates within 72. But cannabis, depending as with all drugs on the user's body weight, and the purity, strength and quantity, can stay in the body for up to 90 days. For that reason, hard drug users are less likely to get caught than those who use cannabis.

Alcohol costs

Alcohol accounts for almost 15 million lost working days, and at £2.4 billion a year, costs industry three times as much as drugs. ■

US tests

The cost of drugs to US industry is now £14.2 billion a year, and drugs testing is now a $350 million business. SmithKline Beecham, for instance, tests up to five million of its employees every year. ■

Signs of stress in the office – a result of workload or possibly drug abuse?

Who says crime doesn't pay?

Trading in drugs may be illegal but it is lucrative. Why do it otherwise? Dealing carries the risk of prison but offers the possibility of large, untaxed profits. If government attempts to crack down on drug use are successful, it could put a lot of people out of business.

The Drugs News talked to two of society's drugs entrepreneurs, who depend on dealing for a living.

Andy, 34

(not his real name) has been selling cocaine for the last five years.

❛ I never thought I would become a coke dealer; I mean, it's not something you exactly plan as a career option, is it? I started out the usual way – taking the stuff myself. I was working as a recruitment consultant and I needed the buzz to network and bring in business. But pretty soon the coke was costing me more than my salary could support, so I got into dealing. Then I started making so much from coke that I gave up my job.

I usually trade in loads worth around £150,000; it sounds a lot, but you'd be surprised how quickly it goes.

Drugs exchanging hands between dealer and addict.

I'm careful who I sell to – only people I know well.

Do I lie awake at night and feel bad about what I do? Not really. It's a living, and in its way it's an honest one. I mean, no one is forcing people to take this stuff. They do it because they enjoy it, it's entirely their decision. That said, I never touch the stuff any more. It was starting to do bad things to me and I decided to kick the habit before it was too late. ❜

Editor's note: shortly after giving this interview, Andy was arrested and is now awaiting trial for dealing. If found guilty he could face life (a 25-years jail sentence).

Evan, 22

is selling cannabis while he looks for a job.

❛ I just graduated in media studies last year and I haven't got a job yet, so I sell dope to bring in a bit of cash and to get myself a cheap supply. I'm not in the big league, just the odd ounce here and there, but I make a fair bit. Two-three hundred quid a week on average.

It started off with just friends, but now the word has got around and I get calls from all sorts. That's what amazes me. The government and police banging on about illegal drugs but so many people smoke dope. Half the people I sell to are respectable middle-class professionals – solicitors, doctors, even teachers. Even a friend of my mum's bought some the other day. Everyone is smoking the stuff. It's the new alcohol.

People assume I'm in favour of legalisation, but funnily enough, I'm not. It's all a matter of economics. As long as the stuff is illegal, people like me can make a killing – you get a load of cigarette manufacturers involved and it'd be out of our hands. ❜

Get Your Drug Act Together

ROCK'N'ROLL'S DRUG CASUALTIES

The high pressure world of pop music and the wealth and lifestyle of its musicians leaves them particularly vulnerable to drug abuse.

A glance at a Hall of Fame of 'drug casualties' reveals the problem only too clearly. Great musicians can find the trappings of fame hard to cope with – or maybe they simply enjoy them to excess.

Either way, the list also highlights the ambiguity of social attitudes to drugs. We don't want our rock stars to

Sir George (right) with the three surviving Beatles.

Sir George Martin, the former producer of the Beatles, has called on the pop music industry to introduce its own drugs code, and ban performers who are known drug users.

Despite admitting that the Beatles smoked 'the odd joint' during the time they worked with him during the Sixties, Sir George, 72, says it is the duty of the industry to lead the way.

However, he does not believe songs with lyrics referring to drugs should be banned – a ban would just enhance drugs' mystique among young people, he said.

Sir George's comments contribute further to the controversy surrounding the pop industry's relationship with drugs. Former Beatle Sir Paul McCartney is a vocal supporter of legalising cannabis. In one interview with the *New Statesman* he said, 'People are smoking pot anyway and to make them criminals is wrong.' Sir Paul himself was famously arrested for possession of cannabis whilst on tour in Japan in 1980. ■

Jimi Hendrix plays guitar – like no one else before or since.

be virtuous and safe – could Noel Gallagher have the same mass appeal if he was a stay-at-home, say-no-to-drugs mummy's boy? Or would the legend that is Jimi Hendrix be what it is today if he hadn't lived a life on the edge, mainly through his drug taking?

THE WILD SIDE

For many of us rock music lets us express our 'wild' side. Through it, we can live a little dangerously. So long as we don't attempt to imitate our idols, we are perfectly safe. But are they? ■

Jim Morrison retreated to Paris to avoid the public eye.

HALL OF FAME

■ **Jimi Hendrix** died of a barbiturates overdose at the height of his fame in 1970. He had also been a heavy heroin user.

■ **Kurt Cobain**, lead singer of Nirvana, committed suicide, but many people think his death was related to his frequent heroin use.

■ **Sid Vicious**, guitarist with punk rock band the Sex Pistols, died of a heroin overdose in 1979.

■ Sixties singer **Janis Joplin** died of a heroin overdose in 1970 after a successful but short-lived career.

■ Rolling Stones guitarist and singer **Keith Richard** had a long history of heroin use during the 1970s. He was arrested 10 times for drug offences.

■ **Noel Gallagher**, star of rock band Oasis, said that taking drugs was like 'having a cup of tea'.

■ **Jim Morrison**, lead singer with the Doors, died in Paris in 1971. While this has been the subject of much rock folk lore, he was known for his heavy drug use in the years leading up to his death or (as some will have it) disappearance. ■

CINEMATTERS

Our resident film critic, Columbia Warner, wonders where movie-makers stand on drugs.

Drugs are cool. At least you could be forgiven for thinking so after a trip to your local cinema. No modern film claiming to deal with the nitty-gritty of life is complete without at least several characters – if not all – taking hard or soft drugs in abundance.

Trainspotting is one of the most notorious, but at least it dealt with the downside. The lethal and unsavoury consequences of shooting up, particularly in the notorious worst bog in Scotland scene, are emphasised as

*Trainspotting's **worst bog in Scotland!***

much as the exhilaration of taking heroin. Even controversially violent *Pulp Fiction* had Uma Thurman in mortal danger from an overdose.

But drug taking seems to be creeping into the mainstream films, in a way that serves more as an advertisement than a dire warning. Take Sam Mendes' recent Oscar winner, *American Beauty*. A fine film in many respects, but it portrays dope-smoking as not only acceptable, but morally regenerate. Indeed, the neighbouring drug dealer could be seen as the most noble and enlightened character in the whole film.

Are these films simply reflecting a social reality where drugs, especially soft drugs like cannabis, are a normal part of everyday life? Or are film-makers seizing on their potential to create a more dramatic and challenging story-line? Perhaps, when it comes down to it, dealers and traffickers are not the only ones making a killing from drugs. ■

Profile

MELVIN BURGESS

The award-winning book *Junk* describes the slow but relentless slide of two runaways, Tar and Gemma, into heroin addiction. Although praised for its honesty and sensitivity, some condemned the book as shocking for including details of teenage drug deaths and prostitution to finance their heroin habit. *The Drugs News* talks to its author Melvin Burgess.

Melvin Burgess

Why did you write *Junk*?
I wanted to share a picture of that kind of culture, rather than get across some kind of message about drugs. My view is that most kids these days will try drugs at some point or other, and they will make their minds up on their own. I hope they will feel able to make up their minds a bit better from reading the book.

What do you think the book says about drugs?
I suppose it says that heroin is a bad thing, because it's true. As for all drugs, I'm not sure.

There are people in the book who do soft drugs and who are responsible and caring. *Junk* is more about addiction than drugs generally.

Where did you get the material for your book?
I lived in Bristol for eight years in that sort of community. I didn't experience heroin personally, but my brother had a heroin problem and so did a number of other people I knew very well. The characters in *Junk* are drawn from real people.

How did it affect you being around heroin addicts?
It's rather mesmerising, and very upsetting. Addiction does make people very untrustworthy. They are always kidding themselves and everyone around them about what they are up to.

***Junk* does show how difficult it is to get over heroin addiction. Do you think many people succeed?**
I think most people do get out of it, although my brother didn't. But it really is a case of 'once a junkie, always a junkie' – there's always the danger of backsliding. It also

depends what kind of person you are. Some people try heroin and don't have a problem with it, but for others it's the most incredible thing you can imagine and they develop a problem. I don't know if that's down to character or weakness or something else, but some people can just drop it, while others will jump into a car and drive 200 to 300 miles just to get a score.

How big a problem do you think heroin is?
As it exists in society, it is really bad and serious, but it's very difficult to separate the problem from its social context. Alcohol and cigarettes are much more devastating in terms of deaths. But I wouldn't say it was okay to take heroin. It is very addictive and the culture around it is far too dangerous, especially sticking needles in yourself.

A Photographer's Eye

Junk **was set in the early 1980s. Do you think drugs education has improved since then?**
On the whole I think drugs education is a lot better – there's much less propaganda and much more information – but there's still quite a degree of hypocrisy. You get the 'drugs are all horrible and bad' authoritarian bit, yet there's all these rock stars and entertainers enjoying them. People were a bit perturbed by *Junk* because it talks about the good bits and people doing drugs for fun, but I think you have to be honest. After all, 80 per cent of people try drugs yet only two per cent end up with a horrible problem. Most people do cope with them sensibly.

Do you think the drugs problem is getting worse?
It does seem to be getting worse fairly steadily. In Bradford you can get a wrap of heroin for just £2 now.

What can we do?
I'm not sure. I think the way forward is in decriminalising drugs, although whether that should extend to heroin I don't know. However I don't see any argument for keeping cannabis illegal. Heroin is different from hash, although I know people who smoke large amounts of cannabis every day and are absolutely useless on it. But that doesn't mean it should be illegal. ■

This picture taken by Gillian Allard shows a drug user injecting himself in the foot, because his arm has been amputated. He lost the arm as a result of injecting Temazepam into it. The arteries hardened and the blood could no longer flow through the arm so it began to rot. The photographer has framed the picture in such a way that, although you see the hook that replaces the amputated hand, you focus on the act of the addict injecting. Without being too gory, it makes the point of how far the man's addiction has taken him.

Shock tactics?

Like Melvin Burgess, Gillian Allard does not seek to sensationalise drug-taking. The picture has impact because it is very matter-of-fact. It simply presents us with the reality of drug-taking without being overtly judgemental. In today's media-weary world, this approach has more effect than the shock tactics used by many photographers when portraying drug abuse. ■

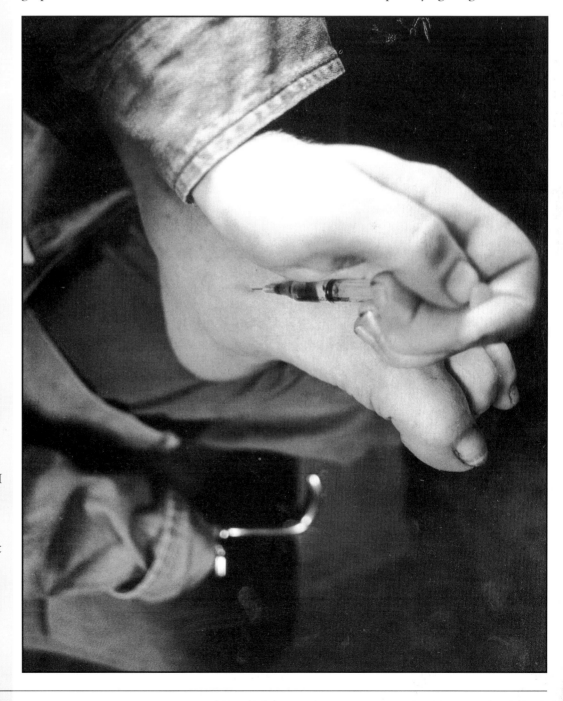

Halt to 'Heroin Chic'

The Fashion Editor

American president Bill Clinton has launched a blistering attack on fashion's 'heroin chic', which shows models seemingly 'high' on the drug and looking thin and drawn like addicts.

'You do not need to glamorise addiction to sell clothes,' says Mr Clinton. 'Some fashion leaders are admitting flat-out that images projected in fashion photos in the last few years have made heroin addiction seem glamorous and sexy and cool... The glorification of heroin is not creative, it's destructive. It's not beautiful, it is ugly. And this is not about art, it's about life and death.'

US experts believe fashion photography may be one of the reasons why heroin use has shifted from almost entirely a ghetto drug used by blacks and Hispanics to growing popularity with the young and middle-classed.

VULNERABLE

Alexandra Shulman, editor of *Vogue* in Britain, admitted that 'heroin chic' photo-graphy may have a harmful effect on vulnerable readers. But she claims that photographers seek girls who look 'spaced out' and unhealthily thin because they wanted to escape the old cliché of pretty models around swimming pools, in ball gowns or outside stately homes. 'I think it is right for fashion photography to be challenging, difficult and disturbing,' she says. ∎

Top model Jodie Kidd with dark-ringed eyes, and skin-and-bones figure.

IN OR OUT?

Do we take drugs because it's fashionable? Some substances have certainly gone in and out of vogue over the last four decades. Here's a reminder:

● In the 1960s, LSD, a hallucinogen, was very popular, along with marijuana. Tens of thousands more, however, were addicted to prescription drugs like tranquillisers, which were freely prescribed by doctors for depression.

● In the 1970s, drugs like amphetamines or speed were 'in'. Cannabis continued to grow in popularity.

● In the 1980s, the number of heroin addicts soared. Amyl nitrate was popular in clubs. Cocaine use increased towards the end of the decade.

● The 1990s saw the rise of ecstasy and LSD made a comeback. Although heroin use declined slightly at the beginning of the decade, by the mid-1990s its use rose as street prices fell. Marijuana's popularity rose to an all-time high, used by the young and middle-aged alike.

● The start of the 21st century has seen ecstasy use fall off slightly. With prices falling, cocaine is the drug of choice.

HEALING CANNABIS?

Will Foster, a US computer software consultant, is now serving 93 years in prison for growing marijuana plants to relieve his chronic arthritis.

Yet many people are turning to the drug for its medicinal benefits. Writer Sue Arnold, for instance, revealed that she smokes cannabis to relieve a hereditary eye condition that has left her almost completely blind. Although research is limited, cannabis does seem to help sufferers from multiple sclerosis, arthritis and glaucoma. But, since doctors cannot prescribe the drug, like Will Foster, many sufferers of these diseases have taken to growing their own. ■

Growing cannabis is illegal, but many people take the risk for the sake of their health.

COCAINE DANGERS

Cocaine is one of the drugs blamed for a four-fold increase in drug abuse deaths in the last four years, with figures showing a fifth of all deaths among men in their twenties are from drug use.

Researchers have recently discovered that cocaine makes the blood more 'sticky', raising the risk of heart attack in users. Volunteers at the University of Pittsburgh Medical Centre had their heart rates and blood chemical reactions monitored after taking recreational doses of cocaine. It was found that the drug also raised the heart rate and blood pressure and lowered the bleeding time – how long it takes for blood to clot a wound. 'The risk of thrombosis, similar to the risk of sudden cardiac death, is real,' says a report in the British Medical Association journal, *Heart*. ■

Don't panic!

Drugs like ecstasy and cannabis increase the risk of panic attacks, says the Phobics Society. The charity, which supports people suffering from phobias, said it was getting more calls from young people who linked their anxiety disorder with drug use. Some were long-term users while others had experimented just once. ■

IT'S PURELY FOR MEDICINAL PURPOSES OFFICER...

Three readers write with their problems to *The Drugs News* own agony aunt, Anne F. Timmins.

Dear Anne,
I think my boyfriend is smoking cannabis. I found a load of cigarette papers in his pocket and I know he doesn't smoke tobacco. He keeps disappearing off with his mates and when we kiss I've noticed his breath always smells of mints. Should I tell his mum or should I simply chuck him?
Alison, 14

Dear Alison,
I think you should talk to your boyfriend first. Ask him outright if he is taking drugs; if he admits it, you can then talk to him about why and tell him how you feel about it. If he refuses to stop, then maybe you should think about ending the relationship. If he denies taking drugs, you will have to make up your own mind whether you believe him or not.

As for telling his mum, I don't think that's wise, unless she asks you directly about your suspicions. It is up to him to confide in her about what he is doing, and going behind his back will not help.

Dear Anne,
I really like going out to parties and clubs with my friends, but several people in our group have started taking ecstasy, and they keep asking me to try some. To be honest I'm too scared. I've heard that it can kill you and I don't want to get in trouble with the police, but my friends just say that loads of people take ecstasy without problems and that I'm being really boring and stupid. What can I do? Jane, 18

Dear Jane,
I think you're absolutely right. Although lots of people do take ecstasy, there is always a risk that it could have serious consequences, and doctors do not yet know how the drug may affect the brain in the longer term. Not to mention the fact that ecstasy is illegal.

Your friends are being very unfair putting pressure on you like this. All I can suggest is that you repeat what you think, and say you simply don't think it's worth the risk. If they're friends worth having, they will respect your decision. If not, you're better off without them.

Dear Anne,
I'm really desperate. Last week I was out smoking dope with my friends, and we got busted by the police. It was awful, they got my parents involved and have threatened to press charges. My dad is absolutely furious. He says I've blighted my future and if I'm convicted I'll never be able to get a proper job. Is this true?
Jamie, 16

Dear Jamie,
I'm not surprised you are worried. This is a serious situation to be in, and it's understandable that your parents are upset. But things aren't as bad as your father says. The chances are the police won't prosecute if this is your first offence, particularly if there is no evidence that you were dealing.

If you are convicted, however, this may bar you from certain careers like law and the armed forces. All you can do is be open if future employers enquire whether you have a criminal record. Explain how you got the conviction and how young you were. Most will understand that it was a one-off mistake and that you have learnt your lesson. Assuming that you have. ■

If you have a drug-related problem and want to talk or write to someone about it, see our directory on page 30 for some organisations you can contact, for example National Drugs Helpline. They'll help you or put you in contact with someone else who can, all in strictest confidence. Anne F. Timmins column is only a one-off for **The Drugs News.**

High in Charge of a Vehicle?

The Motoring Editor

Police forces around the country are urging the government to introduce national drugs tests for motorists. If approved, drivers stopped for erratic driving or a traffic offence may face tests to find out whether they have taken illegal drugs.

At present, the police have no powers to make motorists take roadside drug tests – unlike the alcohol breathalyser where refusing to take it is an offence in itself. Yet driving under the influence of drugs carries the same penalties as drink-driving, including fines and driving bans.

URGENT ACTION

British police want urgent action because in the last 15 years the number of drivers and passengers dying in road accidents after taking drugs has risen from 3 to 18 per cent of total road deaths.

A recent RAC report on motoring revealed that young motorists are more likely to have taken drugs than be under the influence

Car crashes like this one could be avoided if people did not take drugs and drive.

of alcohol. Another survey found that half a million road users regularly take cannabis, 250,000 take speed and 100,000 ecstasy, cocaine or heroin.

In response to these surveys, the government is already planning a television and poster campaign warning of the dangers of taking drugs and driving. Meanwhile the Department of Environment, Transport and the Regions (DETR) is working with government departments in Australia, New Zealand, America, Canada, Sweden and Belgium on the effects of medicinal and illegal drugs on driving.

IN THE BLOOD

Cannabis is the main drug of concern when it comes to driving. Unfortunately, unlike other drugs, cannabis stays in the body for a long time – long after the mental and physical effects of taking the drug have worn off. Although it is easily detectable with a test, it can be very difficult to prove exactly when someone took the drug and whether it has impaired their driving. Police may still have to rely on observation and physical impairment tests to get convictions for the charge of 'driving whilst unfit through drugs'. ■

TRACKSUIT FRAUDSTERS

In the 1980s, steroid use was rife amongst weightlifters.

Sports Correspondent

Athletes could face fines of up to $1 million if they are caught taking drugs to cheat in sport, says the International Olympic Committee, which is planning radical new measures to try and curb the use of drugs by sports people.

But some believe their proposed policies of suspension and fines are not enough. James McDaid, Ireland's Minister for Sport, says drug cheats should be jailed in an effort to clean up the image of international sport. Speaking in Sydney, the site of the Olympics in 2000, McDaid described athletes using performance-enhancing drugs as 'tracksuit fraudsters'.

Others believe the battle against drugs in sport has already been lost. Recently Hein Verbruggen, president of the International Cycling Union, admitted defeat in trying to stop drugs in events like the Tour de France.

CAN DO NO MORE

'It's not just a case of having testing, imposing sanctions and that's it, problem solved,' he said four weeks before the famous cycle race in 1999. 'The problem is that over the last ten years we have moved to drugs that are very difficult or impossible to detect... I'm not preaching for doping use but I don't think we can humanly do anything any more.'

He added that because accepted legal levels of testosterone had changed over the years, cycling officials had almost certainly punished a number of competitors who were innocent. It would be better to focus on athletes' general health, he said, suspending anyone who failed regular health checks.

WEIGHTY MATTERS

However, the International Weightlifting Federation (IWF) would disagree. After their sport was plagued with drug scandals in the 1970s and 80s, the IWF instigated one of the toughest testing programmes of any sport. Tests are taken at every competition and also at short notice out of competition, to stop the use of drugs in training as well as competition.

Drugs are also a problem in the UK's favourite sport, soccer. FIFA, the football world's governing body, is concerned with nandrolone, a common anabolic steroid that increases muscle bulk and body growth.

In recent years there has been a sharp rise in the number of positive tests among athletes, including footballers. But FIFA has decided not to ban the substance, following a study of 148 football players, which found that it was possible, under physical stress, for the body to make nandrolone naturally. ■

COMMON DRUGS USED IN SPORT

Legal

Cortico-steroids: stimulates production of the body's natural painkiller, cortisone, allowing athletes to override pain and train harder. Detectable with careful testing.

Erythropoietin: hormone which boosts oxygen-carrying red blood cells and the ability of muscles to perform. Undetectable.

Human growth hormone: enhances recovery from physical effort and muscle development. Undetectable.

Nandrolone: an anabolic steroid, boosts muscle growth and strength. The body can create a form of nandrolone naturally. Undetectable.

Human gonadic choriotrophin: hormone which stimulates testosterone production, boosting muscle growth and faster recovery from injury. Undetectable.

Illegal

Caffeine: enhances the body's ability to burn fat and increases mental alertness. Banned only in large quantities.

Creatine: naturally occurring endurance and power enhancer which powers muscle movement. Overuse can cause liver damage.

Sodium phosphate: acts as antidote to lactic acid, the chemical produced by the body in response to hard exercise and which causes a burning sensation in tired muscles. Enables athletes to train harder.

Salbutamol: stimulant found in asthma medicines which can increase heart function. Large numbers of athletes are registered 'asthma' sufferers to take advantage of the drug.

SPORTS STARS WHO HAVE FALLEN FOUL OF DRUG BANS

Linford Christie is still fighting to clear his name of drugs charges.

Peter Korda won the Australian Open in 1998.

Diane Modahl: 800 metres runner banned in 1994 for taking drugs, but then cleared in 1995. She is now suing for loss of earnings during her suspension.

Peter Korda: Czech tennis star, stripped of his prize money from Wimbledon in 1998 after testing positive for drugs.

Diego Maradona: Argentinian footballer banned from 1994 World Cup for taking the stimulant ephedrine.

Ben Johnson: the 100 metres champion stripped of his Olympic gold medal at 1988 Seoul Games after failing a drugs test.

Linford Christie: suspended from athletics in 1999 after testing positive for a banned anabolic steroid. He claims his body produced the steroid naturally but he has still to convince the International Amateur Athletics Federation.

THE PRESSURE TO WIN

Competitors in all major sports agree that it is the pressure to win that is the chief cause of drug abuse in sport.

In professional leagues, that pressure may come with a huge reward attached. In the recent European Soccer Champion's League Final, players in the Real Madrid team were promised £250,000 each if they won – and they did. In other sports, fees and sponsorship deals for top players and athletes can run into millions.

Unfortunately drug use in sport contributes to a vicious circle. As more players take drugs to help them reach the top, the pressure on other up-and-coming athletes to take similar drugs increases. However, if some decide to use drugs in order to compete at the top level, they are kidding no one but themselves if they say it is not cheating. ■

WHO'S WHO

The following are some of the organisations delivering information to the public about drugs. The views are varied and we suggest you contact them for more information, ring their helplines or visit their websites.

■ **Crew 2000**
Crew 2000 is a coalition of young people who produce information about how to reduce the risks involved in using drugs.They don't condone or condemn drug use.
http://www.Crew2000.co.uk/

■ **DrugScope**
A leading UK centre of expertise on drugs with links to other organisations around the world. Waterbridge House, 32-36 Loman Street, London SE1 0EE
TEL: 020 7928 1211
http://www.drugscope.org.uk/

■ **The Home Office's Drugs Prevention Advisory Service (DPAS)**
Government-backed advisory service. DPAS HQ,Room 314, Horseferry House, Dean Ryle Street, London SW1P 2AW
http://www.homeoffice.gov.uk/dpas/dpas.htm/

■ **Narcotics Anonymous**
A non-profit making organisation for recovering addicts.
UK HELPLINE: 020 7730 0009
Service Office: 202 City Road, London EC1V 2PH; TEL: 020 7251 4007

There is a world service site.
http://www.wsoinc.com/

■ **National Drugs Helpline**
A freephone number to call for any queries or concerns regarding drugs.
TEL: 0800 776600

■ **Parents Against Drug Abuse (PADA)**
Provides information and support for the parents and families of drug abusers. 14 Church Parade, Ellesmere Port, South Wirral L65 2ER; TEL: 0151 356 1996; HELPLINE: 0345 023867
http://www.btinternet.com/~padahelp/

■ **Re-Solv**
The UK's only national Freephone Helpline dedicated to solvent and volatile substance abuse issues.
HELPLINE: 0808 800 2345.
http://www.re-solv.org/

■ **Scotland Against Drugs**
To combat the escalating problem of drug misuse, the leaders of the main political parties in Scotland put their backing behind this joint initiative.
40 Anderson Quay, Glasgow G3 8BX; TEL: 0141 204 3380;
FAX: 0141 226 5724
http://www.sad.org.uk/

■ **Trashed**
A website where you can get information about the drugs relating to many topics including effects, the law and what to do in an emergency.
http://www.trashed.co.uk/

AUSTRALIA

■ **Australian Drug Federation**
An independent, non-profit organisation working to prevent and reduce alcohol and drug problems in the Australian community.
409 King Street, West Melbourne VIC 3051; TEL: (03) 9278 8100;
FAX: (03) 9328 3008
E-mail: HYPERLINK mailto:adf@adf.org.au
HYPERLINK http://www.adf.org.au

■ **DRUG-ARM (Drug Awareness and Relief Movement)**
DRUG-ARM is a non-profit, Queensland based organisation, committed to the promotion of a healthy lifestyle without the use of unnecessary drugs. It provides resources to assist awareness of drug issues.
GPO Box 590, Brisbane QLD 4001
TEL: (07) 3368 3822;
FAX: (07) 3367 1374
HYPERLINK http://www.drugarm.org.au

■ **The Centre for Education and Information on Drugs and Alcohol (CEIDA)**
Provides information on prevention, education campaigns and projects in Australia, including HIV and Aids, and peer education with heroin users.
Private Mail Bag No6, Rozelle NSW 2039; TEL: (02) 9818 0444;
FAX: (02) 9818 0441
HYPERLINK http://www.ceida.net.au ■

YOUR VIEWS ON THE NEWS

The Drugs News **doesn't just want to give you its views on the news. It wants you, its readers, to talk about the issues too. Here are some questions to get you going:**
■ Should the drug laws in this country be changed? Why/why not?
■ Why do you think people choose to take illegal drugs?
■ Should smoking cannabis be as socially acceptable as drinking alcohol?
■ Is the club culture a drug culture?

■ How do you think methods of policing drug use could be improved?
■ What attitudes do you have towards the people who produce drugs?
■ Why do you think drugs are mainly grown in developing countries?
■ What sort of drugs education have you experienced? Has it been helpful?
■ What do you think about the idea of 'sniffer' dogs in schools?
■ Should all drugs be legalised?
■ How do you feel about drug dealers

being described as 'entrepreneurs'?
■ Should rock stars take a more responsible attitude towards drugs?
■ Should the way drugs are portrayed in films be more tightly contolled?
■ Have you read or seen anything recently about drugs that has affected your attitudes towards them?
■ Has fashion glamorised drug-taking?
■ What would you do if you had worries about drugs?
■ Is it cheating to use drugs in sport?

WHAT'S WHAT

Here's *The Drugs News'* quick reference aid explaining some terms you'll have come across in its pages.

■ **abolition** The banning or legal ending of a particular practice, such as the slave trade or border controls.

■ **addict** Someone who feels a physical or mental need to do something, such as taking drugs.

■ **amyl nitrate** A synthetic drug that comes in a liquid form. It is sniffed. Generally considered a 'soft' drug.

■ **cannabis** A drug made from the *Cannabis sative* plant, which is commonly smoked or eaten. Also known by many other names including marijuana, ganja, grass, dope, weed, pot, resin and reefer.

■ **cocaine** A strong stimulant drug derived from the coco plant, which comes in powder form. It is usually sniffed. Sometimes called coke or Charlie (see also *crack*).

■ **coercion** To force (or coerce) someone to do something.

■ **crack** A crystalline and very strong form of cocaine that is usually smoked. Also known as base.

■ **customs** The controls at ports of entry into a country, designed to stop smuggling and tax evasion.

■ **death penalty** When someone is killed as a punishment for breaking the law.

■ **deterrent** A preventative measure that stops or deters someone from doing something.

■ **economy** The money and trade system in a country.

■ **ecstasy** A synthetic drug with stimulant and hallucinogenic effects that comes in tablet form. Also known as E or MDMA.

■ **entrepreneur** Someone who sets up and runs businesses, often investing their own money.

■ **epidemic** When something, such as a disease or a habit, spreads quickly and becomes out of control.

■ **European Union (EU)** The group of European countries which has agreed to work together by obeying a set of rules relating to everything from farming practices to human rights.

■ **hallucinatory trance** A mental state where people experience an altered reality.

■ **hard drugs** Drugs, such as cocaine and heroin, which are considered more addictive and dangerous than others.

■ **heroin** A drug, usually a powder, made from the opium poppy that can be smoked and injected. Also known as smack and gear.

■ **Home Office** A part of the UK government that controls laws and regulations relating to its own country.

■ **hormones** Chemicals which regulate many different aspects of the body, such as growth. It is now possible to produce some hormones synthetically.

■ **hypocritical** When someone pretends to be better than they are or says one thing but does another.

■ **legislation** The process of making laws.

■ **LSD** Abbreviation for lysergic acid diethylamide and also often known as acid. A synthetic hallucinogenic drug.

■ **magic mushrooms** A variety of small, bell-shaped fungi. They produce a hallucinogenic effect when eaten.

■ **marijuana** See *cannabis*.

■ **methadone** A pharmaceutical drug, similar to heroin, which can be used by heroin addicts under medical supervision to cure their addiction slowly.

■ **monopoly** When a person or organisation is the only one selling a particular thing, and is therefore able to control its price and supply.

■ **narcotics** Substances such as alcohol and drugs that change how a person feels and behaves.

■ **nicotine** A powerful and addictive chemical or drug found in tobacco and most commonly taken through smoking cigarettes.

■ **offence** An action which breaks the law.

■ **opiate** Any drug whose main ingredient is opium, the chemical taken from the seed pods of the opium poppy.

■ **overdose** When too much of a drug is taken, resulting in physical or mental illness or even death.

■ **Prohibition** The period in US history when alcohol was banned (1920–1933). To prohibit something is to ban or forbid it.

■ **propaganda** Information that actively promotes ideas or beliefs.

■ **prostitution** Selling sex for money.

■ **recreational drugs** Drugs taken for enjoyment or as a recreation.

■ **red-light district** An area where there are a lot of prostitutes.

■ **sanctions** Punishments that are imposed when rules are broken.

■ **soft drugs** Drugs such as cannabis that are considered less dangerous and addictive than others.

■ **solvent abuse** The sniffing or breathing in of gases, glues and other chemical solvents found in certain household products.

■ **steroids** Chemicals in the body which help build muscle. Synthetically created steroids may be used in medicine or to enhance athletic performance.

■ **Temazepam** A type of sedative, available under prescription, which can be used as a hallucingenic.

■ **testosterone** The chief male sex hormone.

INDEX